Be-good-to-your-marriage Therapy

Be-good-to-your-marriage Therapy

written by
Kass Perry Dotterweich

illustrated by
R.W. Alley

ABBEY PRESS

Publications
St. Meinrad, IN 47577

Text © 1990 by Kass Perry Dotterweich
Illustrations © 1990 by St. Meinrad Archabbey
Published by Abbey Press Publications
St. Meinrad, Indiana 47577

Library of Congress Catalog Number
89082665

ISBN 978-0-87029-224-8

Printed in the United States of America.

Foreword

Since you first came together in marriage, you and your spouse have probably given careful attention to the practical aspects of your shared life: finances, children and their care, career goals, and home responsibilities. In the midst of all these concerns, however, it's easy to forget that love has a life of its own. Too often, couples neglect their relationship until tiny irritants grow into a serious crisis.

Be-good-to-your-marriage Therapy is a gentle attempt to help couples nurture love and head off troubles. The thirty rules in this book are gleaned from the sound advice of professionals and the tried-and-true experience of couples. The simplicity of the rules enshrines an ageless wisdom that can enable couples, through mutual respect, to live faithful to each other in the presence of God.

1.

Explore life together;
there's always something
new to discover.

2.

Ask for what you want; your spouse can't read your mind.

3.

Compliment your spouse;
be sincere.

4.

Compliment your spouse in front of others; public praise lasts a long time.

5.

Touch your spouse gently; touching says "I love you" in a special way.

6.

Be romantic; never stop courting each other.

7.

Respect your spouse's right
to privacy; individual space
is important.

8.

Don't fear change; change in a marriage can mean growth.

9.

Spend time apart; separate interests generate interest between you.

10.

Play noncompetitive games together; you both win!

11.

Say "I love you"; it's a joy to hear those three little words.

12.

Always look your best; your
spouse deserves it.

13.

Fight fairly; no threats, accusations, or name-calling.

14.

Be willing to apologize;
love means being able to say,
"I'm sorry."

15.

Risk being hurt; love cannot deepen without risk.

16.

Graciously forgive; love is not proud.

17.

Entertain friends; they are part
of your marriage.

18.

Laugh together; laughter can bridge great gaps.

19.

Cry together; shared tears
bond hearts.

20.

Share your dreams; intimacy anticipates tomorrow.

21.

Surprise each other; the unexpected stirs the heart.

22.

Let yourself be weak; marriage is interdependence.

23.

Let yourself be strong; marriage is interdependence.

24.

Do loving things for your spouse; your own heart will respond.

25.

Respect your spouse's family;
you're now part of it.

26.

Look for love; it's there even when you don't "feel" it.

27.

Enjoy silence together; silence
between lovers is sacred space.

28.

Remember the past; your
past forms the present
and the future.

29.

Pray; praise God for the life
you share.

30.

Be patient with each other;
you're still getting married.

Kass Perry Dotterweich is a free-lance author and the editor of *Catechist* magazine.

Illustrator for the Abbey Press Elf-help Books, **R.W. Alley**, also illustrates and writes children's books, including *Making a Boring Day Better—A Kid's Guide to Battling the Blahs*, a recent Elf-help Book for Kids. See a wide variety of his works at: www.rwalley.com.

The Story of the Abbey Press Elves

The engaging figures that populate the Abbey Press "elf-help" line of publications and products first appeared in 1987 on the pages of a small self-help book called *Be-good-to-yourself Therapy*. Shaped by the publishing staff's vision and defined in R.W. Alley's inventive illustrations, they lived out author Cherry Hartman's gentle, self-nurturing advice with charm, poignancy, and humor.

Reader response was so enthusiastic that more Elf-help Books were soon under way, a still-growing series that has inspired a line of related gift products.

The especially endearing character featured in the early books—sporting a cap with a mood-changing candle in its peak—has since been joined by a spirited female elf with flowers in her hair.

These two exuberant, sensitive, resourceful, kindhearted, lovable sprites, along with their lively elfin community, reveal what's truly important as they offer messages of joy and wonder, playfulness and co-creation, wholeness and serenity, the miracle of life and the mystery of God's love.

With wisdom and whimsy, these little creatures with long noses demonstrate the elf-help way to a rich and fulfilling life.

Elf-help Books

...adding "a little character" and a lot
of help to self-help reading!

Happy Birthday Therapy	#20181
Forgiveness Therapy	#20184
Keep-life-simple Therapy	#20185
Acceptance Therapy	#20190
Keeping-up-your-spirits Therapy	#20195
Slow-down Therapy	#20203
One-day-at-a-time Therapy	#20204
Prayer Therapy	#20206
Be-good-to-your-marriage Therapy	#20205
Be-good-to-yourself Therapy	#20255

Available at your favorite gift shop or bookstore—
or directly from Abbey Press Publications,
St. Meinrad, IN 47577.
Call 1-800-325-2511.
www.abbeypresspublications.com